Congressional Research Service
Informing the legislative debate since 1914

Dynamic Scoring for Tax Legislation: A Review of Models

Jane G. Gravelle

Senior Specialist in Economic Policy

January 24, 2014

Congressional Research Service

7-5700

www.crs.gov

R43381

Summary

Dynamic scoring for tax legislation has been discussed for some time. House Rule 13 has required, since 2003, that the Joint Committee on Taxation (JCT) provide a macroeconomic impact analysis of legislation to amend the Internal Revenue Code, or a statement explaining why it is not calculable. The current Senate Budget Resolution (S.Con.Res. 8) includes a similar provision for the Congressional Budget Office (CBO) and JCT. These estimates are not part of the official revenue estimate, but could affect views on legislative proposals.

Official revenue estimates include many behavioral changes, but hold GDP constant. Dynamic scoring allows for changes in GDP. Models for estimating effects on GDP that are used by government agencies and academics are complicated. To those interested in dynamic feedback effects on GDP, these models may appear to be "black boxes." This report, although necessarily technical itself, examines the models used for dynamic scoring, what effects they are reflecting, and how consistent their responses are with empirical evidence. The following points summarize the major findings of the report.

Revenue neutral income tax reform that lowers statutory income tax rates through broadening the base, although assumed by some to spur growth, can potentially contract the economy. The base broadening, by making more income subject to tax, increases effective rates and offsets statutory rate reductions. Models must take these effects into account to appropriately estimate effects of tax reform.

When taxes increase or decrease, some effects that have been estimated may be less appropriate than others to include in the analysis. Some models estimate demand side stimulus effects, which are transitory and can only matter when there is unemployment in the economy. These may not be appropriate to consider in evaluating permanent tax policies. Questions may also be raised about including effects of deficits or surpluses in reducing or increasing investment due to changes in government borrowing. In both cases, these effects apply to spending as well as to tax changes.

Sometimes claims are made that the feedback effects from reducing taxes will largely offset the revenue loss through "supply side" effects that increase GDP and the tax base. No reasonable estimate of the responses of labor supply or savings to tax changes can produce such offsets. The feedback effect from a simple and flexible growth model is less than 10%, given empirical evidence of supply responses, which are small and of uncertain direction.

More complex models for studying supply side effects (intertemporal models), that are based on a more rigid theoretical structure, produce similar results for changes in taxes on wages if the assumptions of the models are consistent with the empirical evidence on labor supply. A review of models currently or recently used by government agencies and academics suggest that is not generally the case (an exception is the JCT's model).

Effects of tax cuts on capital income can be large in these more complex models, reflecting shifting of consumption and leisure to periods far in the future. These shifts, which can induce large short-run increases in labor supply and saving, are generally not supported empirically and may be unlikely. One question is whether the benefits of formal theory in these models outweigh their empirical weaknesses.

Contents

Tables

Appendixes

Contacts

D ynamic scoring (or dynamic revenue estimating) for tax legislation has been an issue of interest for at least the past 25 years.[1] House Rule 13 has required, since 2003, that the Joint Committee on Taxation (JCT) provide a macroeconomic impact analysis of legislation to amend the Internal Revenue Code, or a statement explaining why it is not calculable; the first analysis was in 2003.[2] The current Senate Budget Resolution (S.Con.Res. 8) includes a similar provision requiring the Congressional Budget Office (CBO), with the assistance of the JCT, to prepare a supplemental estimate incorporating the feedback effects into a cost estimate for legislation with provisions affecting revenues that have a revenue impact of $5 billion or more in any fiscal year. These analyses are not part of the official score, but rather provide projected feedback effects, although some may argue that feedback effects should be included in revenue estimates.

Currently, both the House and the Senate tax-writing committees are considering tax reform legislation that would broaden the base by limiting deductions. Some have advocated a revenue-neutral tax reform that allows fully offsetting rate reductions and some a tax reform that also raises revenue. An important issue of debate is the expected effect on the overall economy from a reform of the tax code.

Many uncertainties arise with respect to dynamic scoring, which depend on the type of model used, the behavioral responses built into the models, and assumptions about activities of other agents or supplemental policies that are necessary to solve some types of models. The complexity is expanded in the case of tax reform, because base broadening can also have effects on effective tax rates that could offset part or all of the behavioral effects due to changes in statutory rate reduction.

This report first explains dynamic scoring, including the types of effects incorporated and the types of models used, as well as what groups conduct or have conducted macroeconomic analysis of tax changes. The following section discusses the specific issues associated with tax reform. The final section discusses general issues surrounding the use of various models and reviews the empirical evidence on supply side responses (labor supply and savings or investment) and how these effects are incorporated in current models used by JCT, CBO, the Treasury Department, and academic researchers.

The discussion of economic modeling is necessarily more technical than that in most CRS reports. The first section, therefore, provides an overview with a less technical summary of the analysis and findings in this report. The main body of the report follows.

---

[1] The first CRS report on this issue, *Dynamic Revenue Estimating* by Jane G. Gravelle (CRS Report 94-1000, December 14, 1994, now archived but available from the author) linked the growing interest in the last few years to the greater importance of revenue estimates under budget rules that provided additional constraints on tax cuts and spending changes. For example, the Budget Enforcement Act of 1990 provided for PAYGO rules. See CRS Report R41901, *Statutory Budget Controls in Effect Between 1985 and 2002*, by Megan S. Lynch, for a discussion of these rules.

[2] See excerpt from Congressional Record, 149 Cong. Rec. H3829-32 at https://www.jct.gov/publications.html?func= startdown&id=1191. Other JCT documents relating to macroeconomic analysis can be found at https://www.jct.gov/ publications html?func=select&id=4.

Overview

Dynamic scoring, as a general term, is revenue estimation that accounts for behavioral changes. When referring to tax legislation, the term dynamic revenue estimating is also used. The legislative requirements cited above, however, have a narrower effect since many behavioral responses are already included in conventional revenue estimates. The rules commonly referred to as requiring a dynamic score require macroeconomic effects, incorporating the effects of legislative changes on aggregate economic output. Dynamic scoring as used in this report refers to incorporating those macroeconomic effects. It is often discussed in connection with revenue legislation because tax revisions may cause "supply side" effects (changes in labor supply and savings) due to changes in effective average and marginal tax rates.

How Dynamic Scoring Differs from Current Scoring Methods for Tax Legislation

Current revenue estimates by the Joint Committee on Taxation include a variety of micro-economic behavioral responses that affect revenue yields.[3] For example, increasing capital gains taxes is assumed to cause a reduction in realizations that reduces the potential revenue gain. A variety of other behavioral responses are considered in preparing estimates. These estimates, however, keep total output (i.e., GDP) fixed. Effects on output have been provided in some cases, but are not included in formal scorekeeping.[4]

What Determines the Economic Effects from Dynamic Scoring

The effects of dynamic scoring on revenues depend on numerous factors: the types of effects included, the types of models used, and the magnitude of behavioral responses (elasticities) incorporated in the model.[5] Three types of effects have been considered in previous studies by the Joint Committee on Taxation and the Congressional Budget Office: (1) the short run stimulus effect where a tax cut increases demand and output in an underemployed economy, while a tax increase reduces output; (2) the effect of deficits or surpluses on crowding out or crowding in investment due to government borrowing; and (3) the supply side effects (increases or decreases in labor supply, domestic savings, and net investment from abroad in response to changes in effective tax rates).

There are reasons to consider only the supply side effects since the other two effects also occur with spending changes. There are especially strong reasons to exclude stimulus effects, since permanent changes in the tax code should not depend on fiscal timing. That is, a permanent tax

---

[3] Conventional scoring and macroeconomic analysis is discussed in Joint Committee on Taxation, *Summary of Economic Models and Estimating Practices of the Staff of the Joint Committee on Taxation*, JCX-46-11, September 19, 2011, at https://www.jct.gov/publications html?func=startdown&id=4373.

[4] JCT's documents relating to macroeconomic analysis can be found at https://www.jct.gov/publications html?func= select&id=4.

[5] Elasticities measure the underlying supply side relationship, for example, by what percentage does labor supply increase or decrease for a given percentage change in wages. In some models they are explicit, while in others they must be derived from other parameters.

code change should not be evaluated more or less favorably because it is enacted during a recession. Moreover, the short run stimulus effects may be offset by the Federal Reserve System.

Supply side effects from tax cuts are often presumed to increase output. However, they can either increase or decrease output because of offsetting income and substitution effects. A tax cut, by increasing income, causes an increase in consumption, including consumption of leisure, which reduces labor supply. This effect is the income effect. A tax cut that affects marginal earnings will cause leisure to be more costly relative to consumption which will increase labor supply. This effect is the substitution effect. Income and substitution effects also occur for savings. A reduction in the tax rate on the return to savings, and the higher return, means that one can consume more now and more in the future, reducing savings. This effect is the income effect. At the same time, the lower tax rate (and higher yield) makes the price of future consumption lower and increases savings, the substitution effect. These effects are typically measured as an elasticity: the percentage change in quantity divided by the percentage change in price or income. For example, if the labor supply elasticity with respect to the wage rate is 0.2, a 10% increase in wages will cause a 2% (0.2 times 10%) increase in labor supply.

The projected effects of a tax change on output and revenues depend on the design of the tax change, the type of model, and the magnitude of income and substitution elasticities. Two very different types of models for estimating supply side response are a simple growth model with labor and savings supply responsive to wages and rates of return, and an intertemporal model with a complex theoretical structure in which individuals allocate leisure and consumption over time. The behavioral responses rely on many aspects of these intertemporal models which are not always transparent.

During the budget horizon, labor supply is likely to be the dominant factor, in part, because additional capital tends to accumulate slowly. Output increases when the labor supply or the capital stock increases, with labor supply the larger input. A tax change affects the capital stock by affecting savings or investment, which is typically only 2% to 3% of the capital stock. Even if the saving rate increased by 50% in the first year, the capital stock would only increase by about 1%. Outside the budget window, capital accumulation may become more important and, for some reforms, can dominate the effects on labor.

Special Issues with Revenue Neutral Tax Reform

With a revenue neutral tax reform, where rate cuts are financed by base broadening, the focus is generally on supply side effects, since the effects on short term demand or the deficit and crowding out should be negligible. Moreover, in a revenue neutral change there are no income effects in the aggregate to reduce supply as would be in case in a rate cut alone. If the change is also distributionally neutral any effects arising from these factors are even less likely. Thus the focus of dynamic effects is on substitution effects.

In a tax reform, it is crucial to recognize that the behavioral response cannot be measured solely by statutory rate changes. The *effective* marginal tax rate determines this behavioral response and changes in the income base that change the share of income taxed at the margin also affect this marginal effective tax rate. It is possible for base broadening provisions to raise effective marginal tax rates more than enough to offset the effects of a cut in statutory tax rates, leading to a contraction rather than an expansion in output.

This potential for base broadening to affect marginal effective rates means that it is not possible to project the effects of a base broadening tax reform that specifies the rates but does not specify how the revenue is to be offset by base broadening.

Expected Supply Side Effects of Dynamic Models

When there is a revenue loss or gain or when marginal effective tax rates change there can be supply side responses. The following points can be made:

- In simple transparent supply side models that directly incorporate labor supply and savings responses as indicated by empirical evidence, feedback effects on revenues are expected to be small, in the neighborhood of 3% to 8%. That is, a revenue loss will be reduced by 3% to 8%, and a revenue gain will be increased by 3% to 8% in an overall tax cut. Effects might be slightly larger in open economies.

- More complex intertemporal models can yield similar results with respect to wage tax cuts, if similar elasticities are embedded in the models. In these models, spending must match taxes in the long run, so the results depend on how deficits or surpluses are addressed. An examination of models currently or recently used indicates that many of these models have implicit behavioral responses for labor supply that are much larger than those that are contained in simpler growth models, or that can be supported with empirical evidence. The JCT's intertemporal model, however, has elasticities similar to those found in empirical studies.

- Responses in intertemporal models to changes in taxes on capital income can be large. These models have a rigid structure that causes responses in savings that reflect reducing consumption today for more consumption many years in the future to a degree that is unlikely and not empirically studied. In addition, they cause an increase in labor supply to shift leisure from the present to many years in the future that is also not likely or supported by empirical evidence. One question is whether the more desirable theoretical structure of these models balances the lack of empirical justification.

The remainder of this report provides a more detailed analysis.

Types of Effects and Types of Models

Dynamic scoring normally employs models of the aggregate economy. In some of these models there is a single rate of return and a single type of saving and supply of capital; changes in taxes which affect the rate of return directly or indirectly can lead to additional savings.

These models typically do not address certain features of the corporate tax. Although corporate tax revenues are relatively small compared to individual tax revenues, corporate changes could have significant effects on the overall rate of return. Aggregate economy models capture these effects on savings rates. Corporate taxes, however, may also have more immediate and larger effects on capital, because they may affect flows of capital to and from the rest of the world. This process could occur more quickly than the effects (if any) on increased domestic saving. Most aggregate models have relatively primitive (if any) adjustment for this effect, although corporate models that focus separately on international capital flows exist.

Aggregate Models of the Economy

There are three types of revenue feedback effects:

- short-run stimulus, or Keynesian (demand side) effects;
- crowding out effects of deficits on investment (and crowding in effects of surpluses); and
- supply side effects.

Stimulus effects, such as those in a tax cut, can increase output temporarily in an underemployed economy by increasing income and spending. This increase in demand leads to the return of some unemployed individuals and resources to production. Crowding out occurs because the increase in federal borrowing due to increased deficits displaces capital that would otherwise be used for private investment. The magnitude of the effect depends on how much government borrowing is from foreign sources.

The third type of effect, which is often of the most interest, is commonly called a supply side effect because it refers to the effects of tax or other policies on the amount of labor supplied or the amount of savings or investment (which would affect the size of the capital stock). This effect is more closely associated with tax changes, although it could apply to some spending programs as well. (For example, spending on infrastructure such as bridges or highways would affect productivity, and means-tested transfer payments can affect work incentives.)

These different effects may not be precisely separated (for instance, deficits increase interest rates which can cause a change in savings that is a supply side effect; and tax cuts could simultaneously cause demand side and supply side effects). The three effects can be isolated by sensitivity analysis that includes policies to control for stimulus and deficits effects (as the JCT often does).

There are three basic types of economic models (plus combinations) that vary in whether and how they reflect the three types of effects.

- Short-run models with underemployed resources typically used for short-run forecasting and to estimate short-run stimulus effects on aggregate demand, but not effects of deficits or supply side effects. These models are also referred to as IS-LM models. They can only be solved by assuming some particular monetary policy of the Federal Reserve System. They are often used in the private sector for forecasting and tend to have multiple sectors.

- Basic neoclassical growth models (also called Solow models) with direct estimates of labor and savings supply responses. This type of model, in its pure form, assumes full employment and does not capture short run stimulus, but can capture crowding out effects and supply side effects. Its effects are driven by the labor supply elasticities (percentage change in labor divided by the percentage change in wages) and savings elasticities (percentage change in savings rates with a percentage change in after-tax rate of return).

- Intertemporal growth models, where individuals allocate leisure and consumption within periods and across time. These actions give rise to changes in labor supply and savings responses. These models capture only supply side responses, as full employment is assumed and deficits are offset by some other policy change.[6] The models are of two forms. One form is the Ramsey, or infinite horizon, model where people are represented by an infinitely lived agent.[7] The other form is the overlapping generation (OLG) life cycle model where agents have finite lives (typically around 55 years to cover the working period and retirement), and a new generation is born each year, while an old one dies (hence the term overlapping generations). Agents in intertemporal models often have perfect foresight (i.e., know all of the wage rates and rates of return in the future) although they can be constructed to allow risk and uncertainty, and OLG models can be myopic.[8] Intertemporal models cannot indefinitely have deficits or surpluses, and in the Ramsey model even temporary deficits have no effects. Because these models have a relatively rigid structure, they include a labor supply response to changes in the rate of return. For some tax changes this response to the rate of return may be the major source of a short term labor response.

- Hybrid models, which combine short term stimulus effects with growth models. For example an IS-LM model can be combined with a Solow model. Hybrid models that allow unemployment through sticky wages (i.e., wages do not immediately adjust to changes in demand) can combine with a Ramsey infinite horizon model. In the latter case, some agents in the economy are presumed to be liquidity constrained (cannot borrow).

The alternative models can produce different results both due to the model choice and to the elasticities, or assumed responsiveness, embedded in the model. In addition, some models can (but may not) allow capital flows to and from the rest of the world. In general these models do not include an explicit modeling of open economy effects but may include open economy effects on supply in a variety of ways. For example, an open economy with perfectly mobile capital can be introduced by fixing the interest rate as is done in one variation of the CBO's open economy model. The infinite horizon model, however, is incompatible with perfectly mobile international

---

[6] The offset of deficits is not a choice, but a requirement in these forward looking models, as a solution requires solving for a steady-state or a long run solution that is asymptotically approached. Deficits can exist in these models but they must have a stable debt-to-GDP ratio. An OLG model with myopia can be solved with deficits.

[7] The original Ramsey model was a planning model that was then adapted to the study of tax and other policies in a steady state growth model as a descriptive model. Macroeconomists adapted this model to the study of business cycles due to exogenous shocks, which is referred to as a real business cycle model, which claims to explain business cycles without involuntary unemployment. A term for a more general class of these models is dynamic stochastic general equilibrium (DSGE) models which can be designed to allow unemployment. Tax economists have tended to favor the life cycle form of the intertemporal model, perhaps because it allows distribution across generations that is an important aspect of shifting to consumption taxes. This model is very difficult to construct. Macroeconomists tend to favor the simpler infinite horizon model, in part because they are often interested in business cycles and in intertemporal shifts of labor in response to wage rates.

[8] Risk causes individuals to have precautionary savings which tend to be less responsive to changes in the rate of return. It is possible to construct a life cycle model with myopia, where agents assume current wages and returns will continue and re-optimize their labor supply and savings each period. Other things equal, myopia results in larger responses to changes in tax rates because agents do not recognize the feedback effects of their response on these variables.

capital. Rule-of-thumb offsets against crowding out are used in some of the Solow growth models to assign part of borrowing to foreign sources.

Corporate Models

Corporate models of a closed economy have long existed but they have not generally been used to measure feedback effects. These models, in fact, often simplified the requirements of aggregate modeling because the standard analysis concluded that the corporate tax fell on capital in general, given a fixed capital stock. For purposes of a dynamic model, the corporate tax could then be treated as no different from a general tax on the rate of return. In addition, even though changes in the corporate tax rate could shift capital between the corporate and non-corporate sectors, the corporate tax base would be unlikely to change, because, although the capital stock in the corporate sector decreases with a higher corporate rate, the rate of return rises and these two effects tend to be offsetting.[9]

Open economy considerations suggest that the corporate tax should be considered differently from other types of taxes on capital income. The tax on corporate equity, which is effectively or at least partly a source based tax, unlike individual income taxes on interest and dividends, can directly affect capital flows into and out of the country, thereby increasing output through another route (rather than indirectly affecting the rate of return to savings). Indeed, given the evidence that saving is relatively unresponsive to rates of return and tends to accumulate slowly, capital flows from abroad could potentially be one of the more important dynamic issues to consider.

The Organizations and Researchers That Study Dynamic Effects

Several government organizations have prepared dynamic scores or macroeconomic analyses of effects that would permit estimates of dynamic feedback effects. In addition, a number of academic researchers have constructed models that estimate macroeconomic effects.

Joint Committee on Taxation (JCT)

The Joint Committee on Taxation (JCT) is the most important source of dynamic estimates for U.S. legislative proposals, because it is responsible for official scoring of most tax legislation. The JCT also provides macroeconomic analysis as required by the House Rules and would be (at least partially) responsible for providing the analysis required by the FY2014 Senate Budget Resolution. The JCT has been preparing and then performing macroeconomic analyses since 1997, when they commissioned a number of researchers to estimate the overall effects on output, labor, savings and other variables of the same proposal using a variety of different modeling approaches. This modeling exercise, along with others done over the years, is posted on their website.[10] In their first analysis in 2003, they used three types of models to analyze

---

[9] Certain types of production functions and utility functions indicate a perfect offset and a constant share of total output in corporate revenues; for others the effect is likely small. Corporate taxes produce distortions, but those distortions do not affect aggregate output in a significant way.

[10] The Joint Committee's Documents relating to macroeconomic analysis are posted on its website at (continued...)

macroeconomic effects: macroeconomic short-term effects based on commercial models, a Solow growth/hybrid model, and an OLG life-cycle model. They added a Ramsey model in 2006, but that model is currently being revised.

Their Solow hybrid model (called the Macroeconomic Growth Model, or MEG) is basically a Solow growth model that allows short term stimulus effects, effects of deficits and surplus, and includes a direct labor supply elasticity and a life-cycle treatment of consumption that generates a savings effect. In many ways, MEG could be viewed as a pragmatic combination of labor supply responses, short run stimulus effects, crowding out effects, and a savings response from consumption with the same type of micro-economic foundations as intertemporal models but without the labor supply response to the interest rate. The JCT studies frequently provide sensitivity analysis that allows a separation of stimulus and crowding out effects from supply side effects.[11]

The JCT has tended not to use the short term macroeconomic models after the first study, and in their most recent estimates have used only MEG.

Congressional Budget Office (CBO)

CBO has provided estimates of the economic effects of the President's Budget, which includes tax provisions, each year since 2003. It also provides economic effects of budget projections of different types. Under S.Con.Res. 8, CBO is charged with the responsibility for dynamic estimates, assisted by the JCT.

The first CBO study employed the same four types of models that JCT has used, although they introduced their own supply responses into the macroeconomic short term models.[12] CBO ultimately dropped one of its models (the Ramsey infinite horizon) in its later analyses[13] and did not use any intertemporal model in their recent analysis of budget options.[14] The CBO OLG model has recently been revised.[15]

(...continued)

https://www.jct.gov/publications html?func=select&id=4.

[11] Stimulus effects can be eliminated by assuming an offsetting policy of the Federal Reserve. Deficit effects can be eliminated by assuming offsetting changes in spending.

[12] The initial analysis is described in How CBO Analyzed the Macroeconomic Effects of the President's Budget, April, 2003, at http://www.cbo.gov/sites/default/files/cbofiles/ftpdocs/44xx/doc4454/07-28-presidentsbudget.pdf.

[13] The most recent analysis of the President's budget was in The Economic Impact of the President's 2013 Budget, April 20, 2012, at http://www.cbo.gov/publication/42972.

[14] See Macroeconomic Effects of Alternative Budget Paths, February 2013, at http://www.cbo.gov/publication/43769.

[15] This model was presented in Shinichi Nishiyama, Fiscal Policy Effects in a Heterogeneous-Agent Overlapping-Generations Economy With an Aging Population, Congressional Budget Office, Working Paper 2013-07, December 2013, http://www.cbo.gov/sites/default/files/cbofiles/attachments/44941-Nishiyama.pdf.

Department of the Treasury Office of Tax Analysis

The Office of Tax Analysis (OTA) performed two dynamic analyses in 2006, one on the President's Advisory Panel on Tax Reform's proposals[16] and one on the extension of the 2001-2003 tax cuts.[17]

For their first analysis, OTA used a Solow model, a Ramsey model and an OLG model. The Solow model had a fixed labor supply but a positive savings response to higher returns. In their analysis of the tax cuts, they used only the OLG model.

Other Models and Researchers

The Solow growth model is the simplest of the models to construct and it has been used primarily by government agencies and think tanks to examine the effects of tax changes, largely in the longer run.[18]

Short term macroeconomic models are largely used by commercial forecasters and government agencies, such as central banks; many central banks also have a hybrid model that couples short-run unemployment with a Ramsey infinite horizon model.[19] Some of these models are very complex, with many sectors and interactions. JCT contracts for the use of Macroeconomic Advisers and IHS Global Insight,[20] and CBO relies on these models as well as a macroeconomic model developed by the Federal Reserve.[21]

The Ramsey infinite horizon model is generally straightforward to construct and there are numerous modeling efforts in academia and government. These models are more frequently used by macroeconomists interested in the business cycles and the effects of shocks to the economy, rather than modeling tax changes. Tax economists interested in intertemporal models are more likely to turn to the OLG life cycle model, which can capture intergenerational income shifts,

---

[16] Robert Carroll, John Diamond, Craig Johnson, and James Makie III, *A Summary of the Dynamic Analysis of the Tax Reform Options Prepared for the President's Advisory Panel on Federal Tax Reform*, U.S. Department of the Treasury, Office of Tax Analysis, May 25, 2006, prepared for the American Enterprise Institute Conference on Tax Reform and Dynamic Analysis, May, 2006. This analysis was discussed in CRS Report RL33545, *The Advisory Panel's Tax Reform Proposals*, by Jane G. Gravelle.

[17] U.S. Office of Management and Budget, Fiscal Year 2007 Mid-Session Review, Budget of the U.S. Government, July 11, 2006. This analysis is discussed in CRS Report RL33672, *Revenue Feedback from the 2001-2004 Tax Cuts*, by Jane G. Gravelle.

[18] For example, see Robert Carroll and Gerald Prante, Long-Run Macroeconomic Impact of Increasing Tax Rates on High-Income Taxpayers in 2013, Ernst & Young LLP, July 2012, \ http://waysandmeans house.gov/uploadedfiles/ey_study_ong-run_macroeconomic_impact_of_increasing_tax_rates_on_high_income_taxpayers_in_2013__2012_07_16_final.pdf and Steve Entin and William McBride, Simulating the Economic Effects of Romney's Tax Plan, Tax Foundation, Fiscal Fact No. 330, http://taxfoundation.org/article/simulating-economic-effects-romneys-tax-plan used a neoclassical growth model, but reported effects in the long run steady state, and not the transition.

[19] For a discussion of these models, see CRS Report R42700, *The "Fiscal Cliff": Macroeconomic Consequences of Tax Increases and Spending Cuts*, by Jane G. Gravelle; and Felix Reichling and Charles Whalen, Assessing the Short-Term Effects on Output of Changes in Federal Fiscal Policies, CBO Working Paper 2012-08, May 2012, at http://www.cbo.gov/sites/default/files/cbofiles/attachments/WorkingPaper2012-08-Effects_of_Fiscal_Policies.pdf.

[20] Summary of Economic Models and Estimating Practices of the Staff of the Joint Committee on Taxation, September 19, 2011, JCX 46-11, at https://www.jct.gov/publications html?func=startdown&id=4359

[21] CBO, The Economic Impact of the President's 2013 Budget April 2012, at http://www.cbo.gov/sites/default/files/cbofiles/attachments/04-20-Economic_Budget.pdf.

---

even though this model is more difficult to construct. Because of this difficulty in construction a life cycle modeling has been done by a limited number of researchers. The pioneers in this effort were Alan Auerbach and Laurence Kotlikoff, and their associates, including those who constructed a variation of the OLG lifecycle model at CBO.[22] The JCT and the Treasury both used an OLG model created by John Diamond through a contract with Tax Policy Advisors, LLC.[23]

Special Issues Associated with Revenue-Neutral Income Tax Reform

The Senate Budget Resolution provision was included in the anticipation of tax reform. Some argue tax reform should be revenue neutral, and the House Budget Resolution for FY2014 (H.Con.Res. 25) takes this position. Others believe that it should raise revenue, as in the Senate Budget Resolution for FY2014 (S.Con.Res. 8). Some earlier proposals would have cut taxes along with reform, generally by making the 2001-2003 tax cuts permanent; these proposals would probably be close to revenue neutral currently because most of these tax cuts have since been made permanent.[24] A revenue neutral, or largely revenue neutral, tax reform that lowers the rate and broadens the base is unlikely to have a large effect on the economy. It could contract, rather than expand, the economy, depending on the design.

All of the effects that might be considered in a dynamic estimate, including short run stimulus, long-run crowding out or in of investment through deficits, and supply side responses, would likely be eliminated or dampened in a revenue neutral tax reform.

---

[22] The details of a typical OLG model were presented in Alan J. Auerbach and Laurence J. Kotlikoff, *Dynamic Fiscal Policy*, Cambridge University Press, New York, New York, 1987. A version of their model with additional coauthors Kent Smetters and Jan Walliser was included in the Joint Committee On Taxation *Tax Modeling Project And 1997 Tax Symposium Papers*, Joint Committee Print, November 20, 1997, posted on the JCT website at https://www.jct.gov/ publications html?func=startdown&id=2940. Another more detailed study with more sectors was David Altig, Alan J. Auerbach, Laurence J. Kotlikoff, Kent A. Smetters, and Jan Walliser, Simulating Fundamental Tax Reform in the United States, *American Economic Review*, vol. 91, no. 3, June 2001, pp. 575-595. at http://www2.wiwi hu-berlin.de/ institute/wpol/html/jprof/aer.pdf. The CBO model was initially developed by Shinichi Nishiyama and Kent Smetters, Consumption Taxes and Economic Efficiency in a Stochastic OLG Model, Technical Working Paper 2002-6, December 2002, at http://www.cbo.gov/sites/default/files/cbofiles/ftpdocs/40xx/doc4007/2002- \6.pdf. It includes risk and different types of households. The JCT symposium included two other life cycle models, one by Don Fullerton and Diane Rogers (now Diane Lim) which had multiple sectors and households and one by Eric Engen and Bill Gale, which included risk. Including the discussant Charles Ballard, input was provided from all the multiple generation life cycle modelers at that time. The JCT symposium also included one infinite horizon model, by Dale W. Jorgenson and Peter J. Wilcoxin, along with five models that were Solow-type models or hybrid macroeconomic/Solow models.

[23] John Diamond is the CEO of Tax Policy Advisors, and is at the James A. Baker III Institute for Public Policy at Rice University.

[24] These earlier proposals include Congressman Paul Ryan's proposal in 2010, to extend the 2001 through2003 tax cuts and institute revenue neutral tax reform and the House Budget Resolutions for FY2012 and FY2013. See the Committee For a Responsible Government (CFRB) comparison table at http://crfb.org/compare. Extension of most of these tax cuts occurred in early in January 2013. This legislation is explained in CRS Report R42700, *The "Fiscal Cliff": Macroeconomic Consequences of Tax Increases and Spending Cuts*, by Jane G. Gravelle.

Short Run Stimulus, or Demand Side, Effects

Since there would be no change in income under a revenue neutral reform, there would be no effects on aggregate demand, unless there was a shift in the distribution of the tax burden. For example, if the relative burden shifts to high income individuals there may be a small stimulus because lower income individuals tend to spend more. Likewise a shift to low income individuals would provide a small contraction. A distributionally and revenue neutral tax revision should have virtually no short run stimulus effect.

Deficits and Crowding Out or Crowding In

A tax revision that is revenue neutral would have no direct effects on crowding out or crowding in because there is no change in the deficit. If the analysis extends beyond the budget window, then a tax reform that is revenue neutral in the short run may not be neutral in the long run. Some base broadening provisions (such as slowing depreciation deductions) have a larger revenue gain in the short run than in the long run. In addition, flattening the individual income tax rate structure leads to lower revenues in the long run by reducing real bracket creep (the rise in the average effective tax rate in a progressive tax system as real incomes rise). Thus, crowding out could occur in the longer run.

Supply Side Responses

It is the supply side responses that are frequently the major focus of dynamic scoring for taxes.[25] In a revenue neutral income tax reform, there are no aggregate income effects. There could be effects on labor and saving if there are distributional effects across income classes and if the model reflects those effects, but a distributionally neutral income tax reform would not have those effects.[26] Thus, it is the substitution effect that is the driver of supply side responses to a revenue neutral tax cut. A rate reduction financed by base broadening cannot be analyzed by looking solely at marginal statutory rates. The base broadening provisions which increase tax burdens, and can affect effective marginal tax rates may have effects on supply side responses of labor, savings and investment.[27]

---

[25] See, for example, Curtis S. Dubay, Tax Reform is about Economic Growth, The Heritage Foundation, October 11, 2012, http://www.heritage.org/research/commentary/2012/10/tax-reform-is-about-economic-growth and Dylan Matthews, Why Tax Reform Could Help Growth, *Washington Post*, October 16, 2012, http://www.washingtonpost.com/blogs/wonkblog/wp/2012/10/16/why-tax-reform-could-help-growth/.

[26] In OLG models a revenue neutral shift from an income tax to a consumption tax, a subject that has been a primary focus of modeling using OLG models, can have pronounced effects due both to intergenerational distribution and the timing of tax payments. This type of reform, however, is not the type currently under discussion.

[27] Alan Auerbach and Joel Slemrod indicated that the Tax Reform Act of 1986 left incentives roughly changed. See "The Economic Effects of the Tax Reform Act of 1986," *Journal of Economic Literature*, vol. 35, no. 2, June 1997, pp. 589-632. Alan Viard, in "Statutory and Effective Tax Rates: Part 1, *Tax Notes*, August 20, 2012,pp. 943-947; and Bruce Bartlett, Misunderstanding Tax Expenditures and Tax Rates, Tax Notes, November 22, 2010, pp. 931-932, also make the general point that revenue neutral tax reform is unlikely to alter work incentives.

Corporate Tax Reform

This effect on effective marginal tax rates is perhaps most clear when discussing corporate tax reform. Moreover, in an open economy changing tax burdens at the corporate level is more important for investment (since the corporate tax directly affects international capital flows, while taxes on interest and dividends apply to both domestic and foreign investment). Most of the major provisions that could be used for base broadening in a revenue neutral corporate tax reform directly offset effects on investment incentives of lowering rates. One of the largest, accelerated depreciation, if traded for a statutory rate reduction, would increase the effective tax rate on new investment and discourage investment.[28] This effect arises because the rate cut has a windfall benefit for old capital while accelerated depreciation does not.[29]

Assuming corporate tax reform is neutral in the long run, estimates suggest that eliminating all tax expenditures other than deferral (which affects foreign source income) could reduce statutory corporate tax rates by about 5 percentage points, from 35% to 30%.[30] Out of that amount, two to three percentage points would be due to eliminating accelerated depreciation.

Some base broadening provisions would, when used to reduce the corporate rate, likely offset the rate reduction, with no effect on investment. An important example is the production activities deduction, the second largest tax expenditure, excluding deferral, which would allow a reduction of a percentage point in the statutory tax rate. This provision allows a rate reduction of 3.15 percentage points on profits from domestic production in some industries. If it is eliminated, to finance a rate reduction, effective rates will rise for profits eligible for the deduction and fall for others with likely no overall effect. Although it would not affect savings, it might reduce net equity capital inflows because the industries eligible for the deduction are more likely to be multinational corporations, contracting the capital stock.

Eliminating deferral or other provisions that increase the taxation of foreign source income, which would allow approximately a three percentage point rate reduction, in contrast with accelerated depreciation, would likely reinforce any supply side effects of rate reduction with respect to international capital inflows, increasing investment. This substitution should have no effect on the after tax rate of return or savings.

There are several other minor tax expenditures, but in most cases they would have similar effects to accelerated depreciation or the production activities deduction. It is unlikely that using these other provisions for a revenue neutral corporate tax reform would materially reduce the cost of capital and encourage investment.

---

[28] See Jane G. Gravelle, "Reducing Depreciation Allowances to Finance a Lower Corporate Tax Rate," *National Tax Journal*, Vol. 64, December 2011, pp 1039-1053 and Statement of Jane G. Gravelle Before The Committee on Finance United States Senate March 6, 2012 on Tax Reform Options: Incentives for Capital Investment and Manufacturing Jane G. Gravelle, at http://www.finance.senate.gov/hearings/hearing/?id=7ef25099-5056-a032-52a2-7e15cca1ba5d.

[29] A similar effect would occur if research and development costs were expensed rather than capitalized.

[30] See CRS Report RL34229, *Corporate Tax Reform: Issues for Congress*, by Jane G. Gravelle, p. 40, for a translation of base broadening provisions into the rate reductions they could finance.

Individual Tax Reform

Taxes can cause three supply side effects: labor supply, domestic savings, and net inflows of capital from the rest of the world. Individual income tax reform can affect labor supply and savings.

In a revenue neutral change, there is generally no change in overall income and income effects are negligible. Thus, an analysis of revenue neutral tax reform that relied only on cuts in marginal statutory rates would find larger supply side effects than a rate cut that was not revenue neutral. Labor supply would unambiguously increase from cuts in marginal rates on labor income. In intertemporal models, labor supply also responds to the rate of return. The substitution effect means that, with a higher rate of return, future consumption, including future leisure, becomes cheaper so agents work more in the present to save and have more leisure in the future. This behavior would have a direct increase on output in the short run through increases in labor input and also would cause a larger savings response and increase in the capital stock.[31]

This approach would overstate supply side effects because individual income tax reforms that broaden the base could also have effects on the marginal effective tax rates. Depending on the provision, a revenue neutral change could increase or decrease labor supply and savings since these behaviors are affected by the change in the share of the income at the margin subject to tax.

The most straightforward example of how base broadening provisions could affect marginal effective tax rates is the itemized deduction for state and local income taxes. According to IRS statistics in 2010, the average deduction on itemized returns for state and local income taxes was 5.5% of income for those with an AGI of $200,000 or greater.[32] Because most state income tax rates are progressive, income taxes paid as a share of income would be even higher at the margin. Using an example of 6%, if the federal statutory income tax rate is 35%, and the state income tax is deductible, the total tax rate that applies to the last dollar of income is 35% plus 6% minus the value of the tax deduction (0.35 times 6%), or 38.9%. If the state and local income tax deduction is eliminated or capped, the effective marginal tax rate rises to 41% (35% plus 6%). On average then, disallowing the state income tax deduction is the equivalent of raising the marginal tax rate by 2.1 percentage points for taxpayers claiming itemized deductions.

Although state and local income taxes make this point clearly, any source or use of income that is tax favored and applies at the margin would have the same effect on supply response.[33] The scope of this marginal effect is also significantly broadened when considering that part of the labor supply response to changes in wages is a participation response, which makes the margin for this purpose the average tax on the wage income of that participant. For example, the earned income

---

[31] One study of the effects on savings that eliminated all taxes on capital income and replaced them with higher wage taxes found a savings response in the life cycle model with variable labor that was almost five times as large as in a model with fixed labor. In the infinite horizon model it was about 50% larger. See Eric Engen, Jane Gravelle, and Kent Smetters, "Dynamic Tax Models: Why They Do the Things They Do," *National Tax Journal*, Vol. 50, September, 1997, pp. 657-682.

[32] Internal Revenue Service, Statistics of Income 2010, Individual Income Tax Returns with Itemized Deductions, at http://www.irs.gov/uac/SOI-Tax-Stats—Individual-Statistical-Tables-by-Size-of-Adjusted-Gross-Income.

[33] See Jane G. Gravelle and G. Thomas Woodward, "Clarifying the Relation Between Base-Broadening and Effective Marginal Tax Rates," presented at the National Tax Association Conference, November, 2013, which showed marginal effects for several itemized deductions; and CRS Report R42435, *The Challenge of Individual Income Tax Reform: An Economic Analysis of Tax Base Broadening*, by Jane G. Gravelle and Thomas L. Hungerford, which showed these patterns are likely for many other tax benefits.

credit has been estimated to increase the participation of lower-income unmarried women; a reduction in that credit, even though it does not apply to last dollar, would have a participation effect.[34] The tax benefit of excluding employer health insurance, for example, may not have an effect of marginal wage but could affect a participation response.

A recent CRS report estimated that, for taxpayers at the top marginal income tax rate, a revenue neutral elimination of itemized deductions would leave effective marginal rates largely unchanged.[35] The effect was largely due to the elimination of the itemized deduction for state and local taxes and charitable deductions which tend to rise continually with income.

Some provisions may have marginal effects in the long run but may not induce much response within the budget horizon. For example, restricting the mortgage interest deduction or property tax deduction for those who already have mortgages or homes is not likely to change their choices for labor supply in the short run because the choices have already been made, although it might affect individuals who plan to become homeowners.

Some benefits are marginal in some income ranges but not in others. For example, contributions to employer pension plans and 401(k) plans are more likely to rise with earnings for all but very high income individuals where caps are effective, and thus have marginal effects along with participation effects. An elimination of the child credit would reduce marginal taxes at some higher income levels because of phase outs, but increase them at certain low income levels due to limits on refundability.

The effect of revenue-neutral base broadening depends not only on the type of provision but on how the change is made. For example, proposals have been made for capping tax expenditures, which would leave the increased marginal tax effect intact for taxpayers above the cap but provide less revenue to permit statutory rate reductions. Thus, this change would be more likely to raise effective marginal tax rates for high income households.

Addressing the marginal effects of base broadening is much more complicated in individual income tax reforms and therefore adds to the general challenges of estimating macroeconomic effects. Nevertheless, the message is clear: dynamic scoring that does not take account of these offsetting effects and rests on statutory tax rate changes will overstate the effects of rate reductions financed with base broadening, and possibly project positive effects, when the effects are negative.

General Issues With Dynamic Scoring for Taxes

Tax reform may not be revenue neutral, so that stimulus and crowding out effects could be part of the macroeconomic analysis. Even a revenue neutral tax reform could affect marginal tax rates which could generate supply side effects. This section discusses issues that arise when a tax revision decreases or increases revenue or alters effective marginal tax rates. The following discussion addresses whether stimulus or crowding out effects should be considered and whether

---

[34] Nada Eissa and Jeffrey B. Liebman, "Labor Supply Response to the Earned Income Tax Credit," *Quarterly Journal of Economics,* col. 111, no. 2, May 1996, pp. 605-637.

[35] CRS Report R43079, *Restrictions on Itemized Tax Deductions: Policy Options and Analysis*, by Jane G. Gravelle and Sean Lowry.

the various supply side models are appropriate. It also reviews the empirical evidence on behavioral responses and how they compare with those in some of the current models.

Should Effects from Short Run Stimulus (Demand Side Effects) Be Considered?

As noted briefly in the overview, there are several reasons that short run stimulus effects, which cause a tax cut to lose less revenue than a static score and a tax increase to raise less revenue, should not be considered in dynamic revenue scoring in general, even in models where these effects can be considered.

The short run stimulus effect affects aggregate demand through increased spending due to tax cuts. This increased spending increases output by re-employing unemployed resources (workers who have lost their jobs and idle capital). As some workers become employed and increase their own spending and profits rise, the additional income introduces new spending, which in turn leads to additional production. The successive rounds of output effects are called multipliers. These effects only occur in an underemployed economy (otherwise the stimulus increases the price level) and they are transitory because eventually the economy would have returned to full employment without the stimulus.[36]

There are a number of reasons that this effect might be inappropriate to consider in dynamic estimation. The most basic argument is that changes in the tax code shouldn't depend on the fiscal timing, as tax changes can be hard to reverse. A permanent tax cut should, it may be argued, not be viewed more favorably because it was enacted in a recession.

A second reason for not including these effects, is that they also occur with spending changes. Moreover, spending multipliers are typically more powerful than tax cut multipliers because a part of tax cuts is not spent. If the purpose of the change is to stimulate the economy, then that decision would be better informed by comparing tax cuts with spending increases, rather than considering the effects of tax cuts alone. In a sense, dynamic estimates are already accounted for when multipliers for different spending and tax cuts are estimated.

Third, the magnitude and even existence of a stimulus effect depends on assumptions about the behavior of the country's central bank, the Federal Reserve System. The Federal Reserve can take measures to offset a fiscal stimulus with a monetary contraction or a fiscal contraction with a monetary expansion to keep output constant. They can also fully accommodate the change by keeping interest rates constant and strengthening the stimulus or contraction, or they can do anything in between. If, however, the Federal Reserve has a fixed objective for output, fiscal policy would simply be one more factor to counteract in their policies and a tax cut or tax increase would not affect output. When the JCT does dynamic estimates, it generally includes a case where the Federal Reserve offsets the policy, which is helpful in interpreting the contribution of these transitory effects.

---

[36] See CRS Report R42700, *The "Fiscal Cliff": Macroeconomic Consequences of Tax Increases and Spending Cuts*, by Jane G. Gravelle, which reports the range of multipliers considered by CBO and discusses alternative models.

Should Effects from Debt Be Considered?

There is a somewhat more compelling case that the effects of tax changes on debt should be considered, since, taken in isolation, one could consider the tradeoff to be between financing spending through taxes or borrowing. In addition, if the claim is made that a tax cut will largely pay for itself, then analyzing it as a stand-alone policy including both supply side effects and the effects on crowding out from debt might be appropriate.

The counter-argument to this view is that spending cuts have the same types of effects on debt as revenue increases, so that it may not be appropriate to consider them only for taxes. If dynamic scoring is considered for both spending and tax changes, including crowding out might be more appropriate.

The main uncertainty about the effects of debt is the extent to which debt can be financed by foreigners. If all of the debt was financed by foreigners there would be no crowding out and no effect on revenues at least within the budget horizon.

Note that the intertemporal models (Ramsey infinite horizon and OLG life-cycle) cannot be solved without some resolution of the debt although there can be effects in the interim. A temporary debt that is resolved eventually with transfers has no crowding out effect in the interim in the Ramsey model because it is offset by private saving.

Supply Side Effects

Although there is little disagreement that incorporating supply side responses when analyzing tax changes would contribute, in theory, to evaluating legislative proposals, the case is less clear when these projections provide an uncertain or unrealistic picture of expected effects. The Solow model is straightforward and easily can be used to calculate the expected magnitude of feedback effects. Intertemporal models, in particular, have results that are driven by assumptions embedded in the nature of the model, but which appear unrealistic and have no empirical support in some cases.

A Solow Model Estimate of an Illustrative Tax Cut

The Solow model uses labor, capital and technology to explain economic growth, and in particular to explain observable data such as the capital labor ratio.[37] That is, it began as a model that could explain observations, much as the Keynesian IS-LM models were developed to explain the Great Depression. The Solow growth model was easily adapted to examining tax changes by making the labor supply a function of after tax wages and the savings rate a function of the after tax rate of return.

A simple version of this model, presented in the **Appendix**, can be used to illustrate the magnitude of expected feedback effects. Although the model abstracts from specific features of the tax system, it roughly represents current taxes with a 25% income tax. The results suggest that a 20% reduction in marginal tax rates on labor taxes would increase output in the short run by

---

[37] Solow, Robert M. (1956), "A Contribution to the Theory of Economic Growth," *Quarterly Journal of Economics* (The MIT Press), 70 (1): 65–94.

around 0.5% to 1% and revenue feedback effects would be around 3% to 7% (assuming the capital stock is fixed, a fairly reasonable short run assumption). This estimate uses a labor supply elasticity of 0.1 and 0.2, similar to the elasticities used by JCT and CBO (as discussed subsequently). These feedback effects are relatively minor.

The feedback effects for capital income are somewhat more complex, because it takes a period of time to achieve them. For example, if the capital stock is growing at 3% due to savings, even a 100% increase in investment (either from savings or from capital inflows) would increase the capital stock by only 3%. For growth in the capital stock arising from savings, one simulation showed that by the fifth year (the midpoint of the budget horizon) only 9.6% of the final adjustment in the capital stock had occurred.[38]

To illustrate the possible feedback effects, **Table 1** uses a 0.1and 0.2 labor supply elasticity along various savings rate elasticities to derive the long run steady state. The first two savings elasticities are 0.0 and 0.4. A zero savings elasticity is a central tendency from the literature that used aggregate time series data to estimate the elasticity; 0.4 is towards the larger positive estimates in that literature.[39] An infinite elasticity is provided to show maximum potential long run effects (that is, savings must eventually rise or fall to return to the initial after-tax return).

Table 1. Long Run Revenue Offsets from Supply Side Effects in a Solow Model
Assumes a 25% Tax Rate on Labor and Capital Income

	Labor Income Tax	Capital Income Tax	Income Tax
Labor Supply Elasticity: 0.1			
Savings Elasticity			
0.0	4.4%	0.0%	3.3%
0.4	4.4%	14.5%	6.8%
Infinity	4.4%	48.9%	15.6%
Labor Supply Elasticity: 0.2			
Capital Stock Elasticity			
0.0	8.9%	0.0%	4.8%
0.4	8.9%	15.2%	10.5%
Infinity	8.9%	53.3%	20%

Source: See **Appendix**.

Notes: In each case the effect on total taxes in the economy is considered. Thus a cut in the labor income tax alone will affect labor income tax revenue and also capital income tax revenue.

---

[38] See Eric Engen, Jane Gravelle, and Kent Smetters, "Dynamic Tax Models: Why They Do the Things They Do," *National Tax Journal*, Vol. 50, September, 1997, pp. 657-682.

[39] See Jane G. Gravelle, *The Economic Effects of Taxing Capital Income*, MIT Press: Cambridge, MA,1994, p. 27.

These longer run effects are not very different from the short run effects when the savings supply elasticity is zero. For example, the feedback from a labor income tax cut is 4% to 9% rather than 3% to 7%. Larger savings elasticities can eventually lead to more significant feedback effects, although none is large enough to fully offset the revenue loss.

For budget horizon estimates, it is important to note that a Solow growth model takes a long time to reach the steady state. Effects from labor tax changes in the budget horizon are already close to the long-run steady state. When capital income tax cuts were involved, the effects in the budget horizon tend to be small relative to the long-run steady state (when an effect occurs). In a study of capital income tax cuts with a 0.4 elasticity, on average in the first five years (the mid-point of the budget horizon) only about 10% of the adjustment was complete, and by year 25 only about a third.[40] Strictly speaking, an infinite elasticity would imply immediate adjustment, but such a large change in the savings rate is not plausible, and this is one reason some economists found this type of model to account for savings responses unsatisfactory.

Table 2 shows the output effects for a 20% tax cut, so some idea of the magnitude of output effects might be gained.

Table 2. Long-run Output Effects of a 20% Tax Cut in a Solow Model
Assumes an Initial 25% Tax Rate on Capital and Labor Income

	Labor Income Tax	Capital Income Tax	Income Tax
Labor Supply Elasticity: 0.1			
Savings Elasticity			
0.0	0.7%	0.0%	0.7%
0.4	0.7%	0.7%	1.4%
Infinity	0.7%	2.4%	3.1%
Labor Supply Elasticity: 0.2			
Capital Stock Elasticity			
0.0	1.3%	0.0%	1.3%
0.4	1.3%	0.8%	2.1%
Infinity	1.3%	2..7%	4.0%

Source: See **Appendix**.

Notes: In each case the effect on total output in the economy is considered. Thus a cut in the labor income tax alone will affect both labor and capital inputs. The effects are derived for a small change and evaluated at the midpoint between the old and new rate, 22.5%.

---

[40] Eric Engen, Jane Gravelle, and Kent Smetters, "Dynamic Tax Models: Why They Do the Things They Do," *National Tax Journal*, Vol. 50, September, 1997, pp. 657-682.

JCT has found slightly larger effects for rate cuts in their MEG model (controlling for deficit and stimulus effects) with an average feedback effect of 9% to 10% in the first five years.[41] Their model is, however, not a pure Solow model, but a combination of a Solow and OLG model.

Open Economy Considerations

The model discussed above is a closed economy. The capital stock might change more quickly with an open economy where investment is not constrained by a savings response. The effects would depend on whether the capital income tax is residence based (where the foreign investor is not subject to tax, such as a tax on dividends or interest) or source based (the corporate income tax where the foreign investor is subject to tax). In the latter case, the maximum effect assuming perfectly mobile capital would be the same as the capital stock elasticity at infinity for a small country with perfect product substitution and a source based tax. However, that extreme case is unlikely to occur, since estimates suggest the investment substitution elasticity is closer to 3.[42] Moreover, the United States is a large country, products are imperfect substitutes, and taxes are a combination of source based and residence based. All of these factors would reduce the effects. One study of a ten percentage point decrease in the corporate tax rate (a partial cut in capital income taxes) suggested an output increase of less than 0.2% for an elasticity of 3. This tax cut was a slightly larger percentage cut than the one in **Table 1** and **Table 2**.[43]

Intertemporal Models

Although the Solow model provided a labor supply response in a way that was consistent with standard theory about consumer choices between consumption and leisure within a time period, many economists were dissatisfied with the treatment of savings responses. A simple savings elasticity cannot be derived from underlying utility functions. Intertemporal models were developed to conform to fundamental economic theory about consumer choice by incorporating a utility function to generate labor and savings supply responses. In these models, consumers choose consumption and leisure over time. Some issues arise about intertemporal models of either type, and some are peculiar to either the Ramsey infinite horizon, or life-cycle OLG models.

Some of the initial intertemporal models held labor constant and attempted to study saving in that way. However, modelers also wanted to incorporate labor supply. These models produce results that may be theoretically elegant but are difficult or impossible to support with empirical research, particularly when labor supply can be shifted intertemporally. Moreover, the theoretical requirements of these models require some very strong assumptions about individuals' information. In a typical intertemporal model of either type, individuals have perfect foresight and perfect information (they know how wages and rates of return will change over time for the economy as a whole for an infinite time period of time or a very long time). Intertemporal models, however, can be constructed to include uncertainty, as is the case with the CBO OLG

---

[41] Joint Committee on Taxation, Macroeconomic Analysis Of Various Proposals To Provide $500 Billion In Tax Relief, JCX-4-05, March 1, 2005, https://www.jct.gov/publications.html?func=startdown&id=1189.

[42] For a review see Jennifer Gravelle, "Corporate Tax Incidence: Review of General Equilibrium Estimates and Analysis," *National Tax Journal*, Vol. 66, March 2013, pp. 185-214. A working paper version can be found at http://cbo.gov/sites/default/files/cbofiles/ftpdocs/115xx/doc11519/05-2010-working_paper-corp_tax_incidence-review_of_gen_eq_estimates.pdf.

[43] CRS Report R41743, *International Corporate Tax Rate Comparisons and Policy Implications*, by Jane G. Gravelle.

---

model, which assumes wage shocks and uncertain lifetimes. In this type of model, individuals have precautionary savings which is less responsive to changes in the rate of return.

It is difficult, if not impossible, to incorporate the various institutional rigidities in the labor and savings markets. Individuals in these models can generally enter and leave the work force without penalty, for example, even though in reality leaving the work force may make re-entry at the same wage more difficult. They can change hours even though for many jobs a fixed work week, such as a 40 hour week, is the norm. They can borrow and lend without constraints and at the same rate (although some models have a introduced borrowing constraints for some agents who cannot borrow).

Also, intertemporal models cannot permit a permanent deficit that leads to unlimited growth in the debt-to-GDP ratio; a way to deal with the deficit must be incorporated in the modeling exercise. Thus an intertemporal model cannot be used to examine a tax cut or tax increase; it must be a tax cut or increase and something else, such as a spending change or a future change in taxes, or a lump sum payment, each producing a different result.

Intertemporal models also presume a certain type of behavior with respect to savings behavior that may not characterize actual behavior. Agents in these models look ahead and base their current savings on all of the future periods in their life (even up to infinity). But many individuals either can't or won't behave that way. Some individuals, for example, are young and have no assets or can't borrow, and if they would like to consume more than their income at this stage of their life, they can't, so they save nothing and only change consumption when income goes up. Some because they don't have enough information or knowledge, to operate by some type of "rule-of-thumb," such as saving a fixed dollar amount or a fixed share of income. Others may be at a stage where they want to build a rainy day fund for precautionary purposes, or may be saving for a target (such as enough to make a down payment on a house). Some of these alternative models of savings are discussed by Elmendorf.[44] As noted above, the CBO OLG model includes risk and precautionary savings, along with age related borrowing constraints.

There are also issues specific to each type of model. Since individuals do not live an infinite period of time, the infinite horizon, or Ramsey, model version of the intertemporal model appears on its face to be unrealistic. It can only be justified as a depiction of actual individuals' choices rather than as the prescriptive planning model it was originally developed as,[45] if individuals are

---

[44] Douglas W. Elmendorf, "The Effect of Interest-Rate Changes on Household Saving and Consumption," Federal Reserve Board, June 1996, http://www.federalreserve.gov/pubs/feds/1996/199627/199627pap.pdf.

[45] The Ramsey model was originally a social planning model: a prescriptive rather than descriptive model where treating society as a single infinitely-lived optimizer representing society was appropriate. See Frank P. Ramsey, "A Mathematical Theory of Saving," *Economic Journal*, vol. 3, 1928, pp. 543–559. In a history that is somewhat complicated, it came to be used as an alternative model of both growth and of business cycles. Some economists who were dissatisfied with the ad hoc treatment of savings in the Solow model and some who were dissatisfied with IS-LM type models of business cycles where problems arose through the lack of market clearing prices, adapted the Ramsey model both as a descriptive model of growth and as a model that could explain business cycles through normal market behavior. Basically business cycles, in this view, occurred because a shock that caused wages to rise or fall temporarily caused workers to increase or decrease labor supply. In other words, unemployment during business cycles was voluntary rather than involuntary. This development, particularly for business cycles, has been was criticized by many economists. See, for example, Larry Summers "Some Skeptical Observations on the Real Business Cycle Theory", *Federal Reserve Bank of Minneapolis Quarterly Review*, vol. 10, 1986 pg. 23–27 and Robert Solow, "The State of Macroeconomics," *Journal of Economic Perspective, vol.* 22, Winter 2008. pp. 243–249. Short term macroeconomic forecasting, both government and commercial, remains rooted in IS-LM models with sticky prices and wages, and usually multiple sectors. See CRS Report R42700, *The "Fiscal Cliff": Macroeconomic Consequences of Tax Increases* (continued...)

---

assumed to take into account the welfare of their descendants (who in turn consider the welfare of their descendants, who in turn consider their descendants, and so forth). In general, there is no marriage in these models which could have implications for bequests; agents grow through an asexual reproduction process; in addition, there is no allowance for those without children. The long run elasticity of savings is infinite, so that the after tax return always returns to its original value. It is for this reason that the model is inconsistent with an open economy.

The OLG lifecycle model seems more realistic, although lack of marriage and the presence of childless agents in the models currently used still have potential implications for the savings response (since these may affect bequests). The OLG model, at least in some forms, allows those who are retired to return to the labor force again, without accounting for the unlikelihood of returning to the work force after many years of retirement. This feature appeared in the original Auerbach-Kotlikoff model.[46] Some models, however, have a fixed retirement age, including those of John Diamond.[47] The importance of this feature varies with the type of tax revision, and can be very important in a reform that replaces income taxes with consumption taxes because the loss in purchasing power of income from retired individuals causes them to return to the labor market to restore income through an income effect.

Some of these aspects can be altered. Researchers have had some success in incorporating uncertainty into models, which can account for some rainy day saving which responds differently from saving for retirement or bequests. The Congressional Budget Office OLG model is of this type, although the magnitude of the effect is not clear.

With consistent parameters that produce the same income and substitution elasticities for labor supply, the effect of a permanent tax cut on wages is similar in Solow and intertemporal models. However, the effect of a change in the tax on capital income is different because it will elicit a labor supply response to a change in the tax rate on savings. The change in the timing and intergenerational distribution of taxes when income taxes are replaced by consumption taxes can also have important effects on labor supply, as noted above.

Are the Explicit or Implicit Responses Used in Supply Side Models Consistent With Empirical Evidence?

Even in the same model, projections can differ depending on the parameters or elasticities of the model. Before examining the effects in models, a brief review of the empirical evidence is in order. This evidence includes standard labor supply elasticities (that relate labor supply and savings to permanent wage differences), savings elasticities, intertemporal substitution elasticities, and Frisch elasticities (intertemporal substitution of labor). The first two are relevant to the Solow model, while all enter into or can be derived in intertemporal models.

(...continued)

and Spending Cuts, by Jane G. Gravelle, for a discussion of mainstream estimation.

[46] Alan J. Auerbach and Laurence J. Kotlikoff, *Dynamic Fiscal Policy*, Cambridge University Press, New York, New York, 1987.

[47] See, for example, John Diamond, The Economic Effects of the Romney Plan, August 3, 2012, at http://bakerinstitute.org/files/474/; John Diamond and George Zodrow, The Dynamic Effects of Eliminating or Curtailing the Home Mortgage Interest Deduction, December 7, 2012, http://bakerinstitute.org/media/files/Research/b93d8df4/TEPP-pub-DiamondZodrowHomeMortgageInterestDeduction-120712.pdf.

Standard Labor Supply Elasticities

The elasticities discussed in this subsection are estimates of the labor supply response to a permanent wage change (such as one that would arise from a permanent tax cut or increase). That type of supply response is incorporated in all of the dynamic models with supply side effects. The Frisch intertemporal elasticity discussed below is a different type of elasticity.

As noted earlier, the labor supply response to a change in wage is uncertain in direction because it is the result of a positive elasticity of substitution and a negative elasticity of income.

A large body of evidence suggests the labor supply response to increases in wages is small, varies across workers, and can be negative for men. This small response appears to reflect both income and substitution elasticities that are small, so that even if a tax change substantially lowers marginal relative to average rates (the first affecting substitution and the second affecting income), the response would be small. This evidence includes historical observation, cross section econometric studies, and estimates from experiments.[48] Much of the interest and challenge is estimating responses related to the behavior of married women, where a large fraction of this group does not participate in the labor market. Studies of married women have produced larger, although varying responses. In recent decades, however, as the participation of married women in the labor market has increased, their responses have declined and have become more like those of men. [49]

A recent survey of labor supply responses of men indicated that labor supply was largely inelastic. The mean (average) of the studies was 0.06 and the median was 0.03. The studies indicated a substitution elasticity with a mean of 0.31 and a median of 0.13. The income elasticity had a mean of -0.15 and a median of -0.12.[50] A working paper by researchers at the Congressional Budget Office reviewed recent research and indicated overall a substitution elasticity for men from 0.1 to 0.3, with an income elasticity of 0.0 to -0.1. Married women had substitution elasticities from 0.2 to 0.4, with the same income elasticity range. For the work force as a whole a substitution elasticity of 0.1 to 0.3 was indicated.[51]

One point should be noted about labor supply responses: if labor supply is very responsive in either direction, then it is difficult to explain why labor market participation rates and hours for men have been so constant over a long period of time when both real pre-tax wages and tax rates

---

[48] One study of labor supply used cross country estimates, comparing labor supply in the United States with other countries. This study argued that cross country differences reflected tax rates. See Edward C. Prescott, "Why Do Americans Work So Much More Than Europeans?" Federal Reserve Bank of Minneapolis, *Quarterly Review*, July 2004, pp. 2-13, http://www.minneapolisfed.org/research/qr/qr2811.pdf. Alberto F. Alesina, Edward L. Glaser, and Bruce Sacerdote, "Work and Leisure in the United States and Europe: Why So Different?," in *NBER Macroeconomics Annual* 2005, ed. Mark Gertler and Kenneth Rogoff, vol.20 (Cambridge, MA: MIT Press, 2006), pp. 1-64 attribute the cross-national labor supply differences mainly to differences in unionization and labor market regulations.

[49] See CRS Report RL31949, *Issues in Dynamic Revenue Estimating*, by Jane G. Gravelle, for an extensive review of labor supply estimates. See also CRS Report R42111, *Tax Rates and Economic Growth*, by Jane G. Gravelle and Donald J. Marples, for historical charts and updated evidence.

[50] Michael P. Keane, "Labor Supply and Taxes: A Survey," *Journal of Economic Literature*," vol. 6, No. 4 (December 2011), Table 6, p. 1042. Averages for the total labor supply elasticity (Marshallian) and the elasticity of substitution (Hicks) are provided by the author; the remaining mean and the medians were calculated by CRS.

[51] Robert McClelland and Shannon Mok, A Review of Recent Research on Labor Supply Elasticities, Working Paper, Congressional Budget Office, October 12, 2012, http://www.cbo.gov/sites/default/files/cbofiles/attachments/10-25-2012-Recent_Research_on_Labor_Supply_Elasticities.pdf.

have been changing.[52] Moreover, it is even more difficult to expect a large positive response when historically the rise in real wages in the latter part of the 19th century and early part of the 20th century has been associated with a reduction in the work week. (Women have increased their participation, largely during the 1970s and 1980s, but this change may reflect technological advances in household production, declining fertility, and changes in cultural attitudes.)[53] The CBO OLG model assumes a zero labor supply elasticities (income and substitution effects offset each other) which is compatible with a model where wage rates grow indefinitely. Models that do not have a zero labor supply response have to assume some time dependent change in tastes for leisure versus consumption to be compatible.

Note that while labor supply elasticities are entered directly into Solow type models, they have to be derived from intertemporal models, given the standard form of the utility function (the mathematical expression that yields the tradeoff between consumption and leisure) and depend on the time endowment.

Savings Elasticities

A much more limited literature on savings elasticities developed during the late 1970s and 1980s. These studies used aggregate data in the economy on savings rates and rates of return to estimate the savings elasticity. The evidence generally showed small, possibly negative savings responses. Although elasticities as large as 0.4 and 0.6 had been found, later studies showed these effects were sensitive to minor specification changes.[54] In general, the evidence suggests savings is not responsive to rates of return (a zero elasticity).

Intertemporal Elasticity of Substitution

Partly because of the growing interest in intertemporal models, researchers began to study intertemporal substitution elasticities rather than the effect of rates of return on saving rates. The intertemporal elasticity of substitution (IES) measures the percentage change in the ratio of consumption in two periods divided by their relative prices. For comparing two adjacent periods, the price in the second period relative to the first is $(1/(1+r))$ (which is the discount factor for money in the second period, where r is the after tax rate of return). Thus, the percentage change in price is the change in r divided by $(1+r)$. The IES is the primary driver of savings responses that arise from shifting consumption to the future, and contributes to the labor supply effect due to intertemporal shifting of leisure.

---

[52] One problem with an intertemporal model with an infinite horizon is that either a positive or negative labor supply elasticity is incompatible with a balanced growth economy; otherwise labor would grow to fill all available time, or shrink to virtually nothing. The CBO OLG model, for example, assumes a zero labor supply elasticity (income and substitution effects offset each other) which is compatible with a model where wage rates grow indefinitely. Models that do not have a zero labor supply response have to assume some time dependent change in tastes for leisure versus consumption to be compatible with growth.

[53] See CRS Report R42111, *Tax Rates and Economic Growth*, by Jane G. Gravelle and Donald J. Marples, for data on participation and hours.

[54] These studies are reviewed in Jane G. Gravelle, *The Economic Effects of Taxing Capital Income*, Cambridge, MA, MIT Press, 1994, p. 27. The most recent study was Jonathan Skinner and Daniel Feenberg, "The Impact of the 1986 Tax Reform on Personal Saving," in *Do Taxes Matter? The Impact of the Tax Reform Act of 1986*, Ed. Joel Slemrod, Cambridge MA: The MIT Press, 1990.

Empirical studies have looked at changes in macroeconomic consumption aggregates in some cases and have used individual consumption behavior in others to estimate the elasticity. The pioneering study of intertemporal substitution elasticities was by Robert Hall,[55] who found that the elasticity was extremely small, could be zero, was statistically insignificant and was no more than 0.2. Early surveys of the value led to the use of elasticities of 0.25 to 0.33.[56] Most subsequent studies produced elasticities below 0.5, although some very large ones were estimated.

Recently a large meta-analysis (an analysis that combines data from many studies) of estimates of the IES across many countries found an overall elasticity of 0.5 for the world on average and 0.6 for the United States was prepared.[57] About half the 169 studies were based on U.S. data. The authors cautioned that the estimates were aimed at comparing across countries and were too large in value because of publication bias. Publication bias is a problem widely recognized in many fields. Basically if theory indicates an elasticity should be positive, and the estimate is negative, peer reviewers are less likely to recommend publication, editors are less likely to publish, and researchers, expecting the unlikelihood of publishing, tend not to submit their articles (which often involve a fee), or even prepare a working paper. Yet, when a large number of estimates have been made, because of the fundamental theory of statistical estimation, some would be negative (particularly if the true value is low). Publication bias also suggests that estimates of the income and substitution elasticities are probably too large in absolute value.

One of the co-authors of this meta-analysis subsequently published the basic (worldwide) results after correcting for estimated publication bias.[58] The correction indicates that the elasticity for macro aggregate studies is zero (as Hall originally found). In the basic case (without selecting across studies for other characteristics) the elasticity for micro studies (which were about a quarter of the studies) was 0.22. He also reported that the elasticity for micro studies of asset holders was 0.36. His preferred estimate with various other characteristics selected was 0.33 for asset holders. In general, an IES for asset holders would be only appropriate if the model identified a separate group of liquidity constrained consumers. For a model without that feature the elasticity for asset holders would be too high. If the macro elasticities were considered as well as micro, then an IES of zero to 0.2 might be in order.

Note also that other types of estimates discussed in this section, including the estimates of standard labor substitution elasticities already reviewed and the intertemporal labor supply

---

[55] Robert E. Hall, R.E., "Intertemporal Substitution in Consumption," *Journal of Political Economy,* vol. 96, no. 2, April 1988, pp. 339–357.

[56] Auerbach and Kotlikoff report the results of nine different studies which ranged in value from less than 0.1 to more than 1. The median value was around 0.3 and a weighted average of eight of them using the mid-point of each range (and excluding a study by Mankiw, Rotemberg and Summers in which it is clear the authors were not very satisfied with the model) yielded an estimate of 0.39. See Alan J. Auerbach and Laurence J. Kotlikoff, *Dynamic Fiscal Policy,* Cambridge University Press, New York, New York, 1987. They adopt a value of 0.25. Elmendorf undertakes a survey of the studies most commonly cited and obtains a weighted average of 0.37; he uses 0.33 in his work. See Douglas W. Elmendorf, "The Effect of Interest-Rate Changes on Household Saving and Consumption," Federal Reserve Board, June 1996, http://www.federalreserve.gov/pubs/feds/1996/199627/199627pap.pdf.

[57] C Tomas Havraneka, Roman Horvathb, Zuzana Irsovab, and Marek Rusnaka, Cross-Country Heterogeneity in Intertemporal Substitution, Institute of Economic Studies, Faculty of Social Sciences, Charles University in Prague, http://ies.fsv.cuni.cz/sci/publication/show/id/4868/lang/cs. A meta-analysis does not simply average results of studies but weights them according to the number of observations and sometimes by confidence intervals.

[58] Tomas Havranek, Publication Bias in Measuring Intertemporal Substitution, Czech National Bank and Charles University, Prague, September 16, 2013, http://meta-analysis.cz/eis/eis.pdf.

---

elasticities discussed subsequently, may also be affected by publication bias, since they included only estimates in the direction expected by theory.

There are two caveats about the empirical evidence on the IES for consumption. The first is that the estimates have considered periods that are close together, but the elasticity in models is applied over many periods of time and is determined by a utility function that assumes a constant elasticity of substitution. Most of the effect on savings from a change in the tax rate on capital income arises from reducing current consumption to shift it to these periods further into the future. Yet, basic economic theory suggests elasticities are higher for closer substitutes, and close together periods would be expected to be closer substitutes than further apart periods. Thus the IES estimate should be an upper bound.

The second, and perhaps more important, concern for effects in the budget horizon, is that due to the nature of the utility function, leisure also responds to changes in the rate of return, which then generates a significant short run labor supply response. No empirical evidence supports this response, which can dominate the effects when taxes on capital income are cut deeply.[59] Ballard, a discussant of the intertemporal model simulations carried out by the JCT stated "Any simulation model that generates a large elasticity of labor supply with respect to the interest rate is shooting in the dark."[60] Ballard believes that the controlling of the response of labor supply to interest rates is crucial to modeling and that this can be achieved, in part, via the time endowment (limiting the available supply of leisure).

Frisch (Intertemporal Labor Substitution Elasticity with Respect to Wages)

The Frisch elasticity, which estimates the response of workers to changes in the wage rate over time, is not likely to be of importance in an analysis of a permanent tax change.[61] It is, however, a parameter that has been estimated and can be compared with the implied elasticities in the intertemporal models. As is the case with standard labor supply estimates, it is calculated from other parameters in intertemporal models.

There are two types of estimates. Some are from micro data studies that examine individual behavior over time. These elasticities tend to be small, on the whole, at least for men. There are also estimates from aggregate micro data, which tend to be large, usually above 1 or 2. These macroeconomic estimates are largely based on variations in hours and wages over the business cycle. They rest on the assumption that unemployment during recessions is voluntary, while most models of business cycles consider workers who lose their jobs or have their hours reduced are largely involuntarily unemployed or underemployed.[62] Assuming some or most of unemployment is involuntary, these estimates overstate the Frisch elasticity.

---

[59] In simulations of intertemporal models where a consumption tax was substituted for an income tax in a revenue neutral change and the wage tax actually increased, labor supply increased by significant amounts throughout the first ten years and dominated the change in output. See Eric Engen, Jane Gravelle, and Kent Smetters, "Dynamic Tax Models: Why They Do the Things They Do," *National Tax Journal*, Vol. 50, September, 1997, pp. 657-682.

[60] Comment by Charles Ballard, Joint Committee On Taxation, *Tax Modeling Project And 1997 Tax Symposium Papers*, Joint Committee Print, November 20, 1997, posted on the JCT website at https://www.jct.gov/ publications html?func=startdown&id=2940.

[61] An exception would be where a tax cut today is offset by a tax cut in the future as a way of dealing with the requirement that deficits must be offset in intertemporal models.

[62] See CRS Report R42700, *The "Fiscal Cliff": Macroeconomic Consequences of Tax Increases and Spending Cuts*, by (continued...)

The micro data studies largely concentrate on the response of hours of work and examine the response with profiles of wages and hours over time. Both show an inverted U shape, with fewer hours when young and when old, and lower wages when young and old, respectively, but the shapes are quite different, which leads to lower elasticities.[63]

Turning to the microeconomic data, Keane also surveyed the Frisch elasticity studies for men for hours of work. He lists 13 studies with a mean elasticity of 0.85. The estimate, however, was greatly influenced by one outlier (of 6.25); with that study excluded, the mean was 0.4. The median value was 0.31 although six of the studies had values clustered between 0.03 and 0.17, while the others varied substantially. CBO researchers recently examined the Frisch estimates.[64] They relied on microeconomic evidence. As discussed in their paper, the few studies of Frisch elasticities for married women tend to be higher than those of men. The elasticity estimates for women also appear to be declining, consistent with other work that shows married women's labor supply response is becoming more like that of men. The paper also reviews labor force participation elasticities, where studies have been focused on those close to retirement. Overall, the authors suggest a range of the Frisch elasticity from 0.27 to 0.53, with a central estimate of 0.4. Neither of these studies reference Ball, who found a zero Frisch elasticity.[65] For Keane's summary, including this study would reduce the mean to 0.34 and the median to 0.17.

A Note on Time Endowments

One of the most important, and yet often largely overlooked, parameters that affect the labor supply response in intertemporal models used to analyze taxes is the time endowment.[66] Because choices are made with a utility function where individuals choose leisure and consumption, leisure demand has to be translated into labor supply, and the correspondence between those two drives the relationship.[67] A larger time endowment, which allows a larger amount of leisure, causes all of the labor supply elasticities to be larger.

(...continued)

Jane G. Gravelle, for a further discussion of differences in macroeconomic models.

[63] A number of studies have criticized either smaller or larger Frisch elasticities on a variety of grounds. For example, Keane and Rogers argue that the low elasticities in micro studies for men could be higher if human capital formation were considered, although responses to transitory effects would be smaller than the response to permanent changes in the wage profile. See Michael Keane and Richard Rogerson, "Micro and Macro Labor Supply Elasticities: An Assessment of Conventional Wisdom," *Journal of Economic Literature*, vol. 50, no. 2 (June 2012), pp. 464-476. Card, however, questions even the small elasticities. He provides diagrams showing wage patterns of those with elementary, high school and college educations They show very different patterns of wage growth (i.e., wages of college graduates tend to rise initially and for some extended period of time, while wages of those with elementary education change very little). These groups have very similar lifetime working profiles. This evidence suggests that there is little relationship between wages and work effort; rather men begin working when they finish schooling and reduce hours slightly when they get older. David Card, "Intertemporal Labor Supply: An Assessment," in Christopher Sims, (ed.), *Advances in Econometrics*, Sixth World Congress, New York, Cambridge University Press, 1994.

[64] Felix Reichling and Charles Whalen, Review of Estimates of the Frisch Elasticity of Labor Supply, Working Paper 2012-13. October 2012, http://www.cbo.gov/sites/default/files/cbofiles/attachments/10-25-2012-Frisch_Elasticity_of_Labor_Supply.pdf.

[65] Laurence Ball, "Intertemporal Substitution and Constraints on Labor Supply: Evidence from Panel Data," *Economic Inquiry*, vol. 8, no. 4 (October 1990), pp. 706-724.

[66] This time endowment is effectively set by setting the shares of leisure and consumption in the utility function. Since consumption and labor are known, this parameter sets the amount of leisure and the total time endowment.

[67] Some models enter labor as part of a negative additive utility and there is no time endowment issue, but that is not the case with the models in **Table 4**.

If this measure is set independently, there are no obvious guides to how big it should be. A 40 hour work week is 24% of the total hours in a week, and the leisure share is 76%. There is, however, a biological need to sleep. If a 40 hour week is assumed, and 8 hours per day are assigned to sleep, the share of leisure would be 64%. However, workers may have an embedded lunch hour, and spend some necessary time commuting (which is like working, in that it provides benefits such as lower housing prices), household activities, and care of family members. The American Time Use Survey indicates that the ratio of leisure to the sum of leisure and work is 43% for men aged 35 to 44 and 47% for women in the same age range. These numbers tend to be relatively steady throughout the primary working age of 25 to 54 for both groups.[68] On average men between ages 35 and 44 work 42 hours a week and women work 29 hours (reflecting some of those who are not in the work force). Women, however, spend much more time than men on house work and care of family members.

Another way of considering this issue is that if it were assumed that the ratio of a leisure to hours available for a full time worker is 0.5, then that person would be effectively able to hold two jobs (work 80 hours a week) which would imply 10 to 12 hour work days every day. If it were assumed that up to another half time job could be taken, then a ratio of 0.33 would be appropriate.

The first study by Auerbach and Kotlikoff set the time endowment at 5,000 hours a year, which would lead to a leisure share of time at 0.6 assuming working for 40 hours for 50 weeks (2,000 hours).[69] In another early study, Fullerton and Rogers set the time endowment at 4,000 hours, which would suggest a share of 0.5.[70] According to current data average hours are 42.5 for those who usually work full time and 38.5 for all workers.[71] Neither study had a discussion of the basis for their choice. Current or recently used models range from a 0.3 to a 0.6 ratio of leisure to hours available.

Comparing Empirical Estimates to Estimates in the Models

This section examines the estimates used in the models (primarily JCT, CBO, and Treasury). To summarize the review, the evidence suggests that the labor income elasticity is between 0.0 and minus 0.1, the substitution elasticity between 0.0 and 0.3, total labor supply elasticity less than 0.3, the savings rate elasticity around zero but no more than 0.4 if positive, the intertemporal substitution elasticity should be 0.2 or less, and the Frisch elasticity 0.5 or less. Note that except for the intertemporal substitution elasticity none of these estimates have been adjusted for publication bias, and thus would probably be smaller in absolute value.

Table 3 shows the values in the Solow models. The labor income and substitution elasticities in all three models are consistent with the empirical estimates noted above. The Treasury study is low on the elasticities for labor income and substitution effects; it is also toward the high end on the savings elasticity. All of these estimates are inside the ranges suggested above, with a labor substitution elasticity of less than 0.3. Note, however, that even a limited difference can have an

---

[68] U.S. Department of Labor, American Time Use Survey, Table 3, http://www.bls.gov/news release/atus.t03 htm.

[69] Alan J. Auerbach and Laurence J. Kotlikoff, *Dynamic Fiscal Policy*, Cambridge University Press, New York, New York, 1987.

[70] Don Fullerton and Diane Lim Rogers, *Who Bears the Lifetime Tax Burden*, Washington, DC, The Brookings Institution, 1993.

[71] U.S. Department of Labor, Household Data, Annual Averages, Table 19. Persons at Work in Agriculture and Non-Agriculture Industries by Hours of Work, 2012.

impact, so that a change that cut marginal and average rates the same amount would have twice the effect in the CBO model as in the JCT model. Note also that the JCT model is not a pure Solow model, but rather has an intertemporal model of consumption over time.

Table 3. Supply Elasticities in Solow Models

Elasticity	Joint Committee on Taxation (JCT)	Congressional Budget Office (CBO)	Treasury
Labor Income	-0.10	-0.05	0.00
Labor Substitution	0.20	0.24	0.00
Total Labor	0.10	0.19	0.00
Savings	NA	0.20	0.40

Source: Joint Committee on Taxation, Macroeconomic Analysis Of Various Proposals To Provide $500 Billion In Tax Relief , February 2013,JCX-4-05, March 01, 2005, at https://www.jct.gov/publications.html?func= startdown&id=1189; Congressional Budget Office, The 2013 Long Term Budget Outlook, September 2013, p. 82, http://www.cbo.gov/sites/default/files/cbofiles/attachments/44521-LTBO2013_0.pdf; Robert Carroll, John Diamond, Craig Johnson, and James Makie III, A Summary of the Dynamic Analysis of the Tax Reform Options Prepared for the President's Advisory Panel on Federal Tax Reform, U.S. Department of the Treasury, Office of Tax Analysis, May 25, 2006, prepared for the American Enterprise Institute Conference on Tax Reform and Dynamic Analysis, May, 2006.

Notes: The JCT model uses a life cycle consumption approach to savings with an IES of 0.25 and indicates that the long run elasticity is 0.29. Presumably the adjustment is more rapid than in a standard Solow model. JCT and CBO also provide sensitivity analysis with labor supply elasticities, Their lifecycle elasticity appears to be slightly higher than that suggested in the meta-analysis.

The elasticities in the intertemporal model must be derived in some cases. The parameters that are directly entered into a model that has a utility function composed of leisure and consumption, are the intertemporal elasticity of substitution (over time), the intratemporal substitution between leisure and consumption, and leisure as a share of time (which is set by the value of coefficients on leisure and consumption in the utility function).

To convert leisure demand into labor supply, the substitution elasticity and income elasticity for leisure (which is one because of the nature of the utility function) must be multiplied by the ratio of leisure to hours available (assuming there is no other non-labor income).[72] The Frisch elasticity is the ratio of leisure to labor, multiplied by a weighted average of the intertemporal and the intratemporal substitution elasticities (with the weights the shares of leisure and consumption). The other intertemporal elasticity of labor supply (the change in labor as the relative price of future consumption changes through changes in the rate of return) is the ratio of leisure to labor, multiplied by the intertemporal substitution elasticity.

Table 4 reports both these direct and derived elasticities for the JCT, CBO, and Treasury models along with assumptions made in two academic studies of taxation that use an OLG model. Note

---

[72] The values change slightly with income used for consumption, which raises the substitution elasticity and lowers the income elasticity. For example the JCT implied elasticity would be 0.17 if 25% of consumption came from other sources and the incomes elasticity would be 0.27 rather than 0.30. See CRS Report RL31949, *Issues in Dynamic Revenue Estimating*, by Jane G. Gravelle, for the conversion formulas.

that only one model in **Table 4** is a Ramsey model (the Treasury model).[73] As indicated in **Table 4**, in contrast to the Solow models the implied labor substitution elasticities are higher those empirically estimated in the CBO, the Treasury Ramsey model and the Diamond tax reform. A large part of the reason for this high elasticity is the large leisure share of time, although they also tend to have larger substitution elasticities. All of the income elasticities are too large in absolute value and all of the models except CBO have a backward bending labor supply (in contrast to the Solow models). The largest absolute values are in the Treasury Ramsey and Diamond Tax Reform model, with the lowest in the JCT and Diamond Zodrow study. Since the form of the utility function forces the income elasticity of demand for leisure to be one, these values are driven by the leisure share of time. Compared to empirical estimates, the Frisch elasticity is too high in the Treasury Ramsey model, slightly low in the JCT model and in a general range in the rest of the models. Finally, the last elasticity, the intertemporal labor supply response to the interest rate should probably be close to zero since there is no evidence supporting any response. They are largest in the Treasury models and the Diamond Tax Reform study.

Table 4. Elasticities and Parameters in Intertemporal Models

Parameter or Elasticity	Joint Committee on Taxation, OLG	Congressional Budget office, OLG	Treasury Ramsey Model	Treasury OLG Model	Diamond Study of Tax Reform OLG	Diamond Zodrow Study, OLG
Intertemporal Substitution Elasticity	0.25	0.33	0.25	0.35	0.50	0.30
Intratemporal Substitution Elasticity	0.50	1.00	0.80	0.60	0.80	0.80
Leisure Share	0.30	0.39	0.60	0.50	0.45	0.30
Implied Labor Substitution Elasticity	0.15	0.39	0.48	0.30	0.36	0.24
Implied Labor Income Elasticity	-0.30	-0.39	-0.60	-0.5	-0.45	-0.30
Implied Frisch (Intertemporal Labor Supply With Respect to Wages Holding Interest Rates Constant)	0.18	0.50	0.71	0.48	0.54	0.28

[73] A working paper discussed the parameters of the CBO Ramsey model. Its principal difference from the CBO OLG model was assuming a leisure share of hours of 0.5, rather than 0.4, which increases the elasticities. See Maria I. Marika Santoro The CBO Infinite-Horizon Model with Idiosyncratic Uncertainty and Borrowing Constraints, Working Paper 2009-3, October 2009. http://www.cbo.gov/sites/default/files/cbofiles/ftpdocs/106xx/doc10683/2009-03.pdf.

Parameter or Elasticity	Joint Committee on Taxation, OLG	Congressional Budget office, OLG	Treasury Ramsey Model	Treasury OLG Model	Diamond Study of Tax Reform OLG	Diamond Zodrow Study, OLG
Implied Intertemporal Labor Supply Elasticity With Respect to Prices Holding Wage Rate Constant	0.11	0.21	0.38	0.35	0.41	0.13

Source: Joint Committee on Taxation, Macroeconomic Analysis Of Various Proposals To Provide $500 Billion In Tax Relief , February 2013,JCX-4-05, March 01, 2005, at https://www.jct.gov/publications.html?func= startdown&id=1189; Shinichi Nishiyama, Fiscal Policy Effects in a Heterogeneous-Agent Overlapping-Generations Economy With an Aging Population, Congressional Budget Office, Working Paper 2013-07, December 2013 at http://www.cbo.gov/sites/default/files/cbofiles/attachments/44941-Nishiyama.pdf, Robert Carroll, John Diamond, Craig Johnson, and James Makie III, A Summary of the Dynamic Analysis of the Tax Reform Options Prepared for the President's Advisory Panel on Federal Tax Reform, U.S. Department of the Treasury, Office of Tax Analysis, May 25, 2006, prepared for the American Enterprise Institute Conference on Tax Reform and Dynamic Analysis, May, 2006. John Diamond, The Economic Effects of the Romney Plan, August 3, 2012 at http://bakerinstitute.org/files/474/. John Diamond and George Zodrow, The Dynamic Effects of Eliminating or Curtailing the Home Mortgage Interest Deduction, December 7, 2012, http://bakerinstitute.org/media/files/Research/b93d8df4/TEPP-pub-DiamondZodrowHomeMortgageInterestDeduction-120712.pdf. Formulas for converting the first three parameters in supply elasticities can be found in CRS Report RL31949, *Issues in Dynamic Revenue Estimating*, by Jane G. Gravelle, Appendix C. Note that some of the information used to obtain estimates was provided directly by the authors and does not appear in the publications.

Notes: Implied labor substitution and income elasticities are calculated assuming only wage income. If capital income exists, the substitution elasticity elasticities would be higher.

Is it possible to make choices that would lead to better outcomes (although the JCT model does fairly well at being consistent with most values in the empirical literature)? It would require using the time endowment as a tool to fit the model to evidence, as suggested by Ballard. For example, set the intertemporal elasticity at 0.2, consistent with the evidence. Set the intratemporal substitution elasticity at 1.5 and the leisure share of hours at 0.15. Then the labor substitution elasticity would be 0.225, the income elasticity would be -0.15, and there would be a slight positive elasticity of total labor supply. The Frisch elasticity would be 0.23 (using labor and leisure shares as proxies for shares of consumption and leisure), at the low end, but reasonable considering publication bias, and the elasticity of labor with response to price change would be 0.026, small enough not to be very troubling.

Note that the CBO model is a model with uncertainty. Generally, uncertainty should lead to precautionary savings that is not sensitive to the interest rate, and a lower savings response.[74]

---

[74] Engen, Gravelle, and Smetters included a comparison of a myopic OLG model with fixed labor with and without uncertainty. Introducing uncertainty reduced the effects by more than half. However, that may not be similar with endogenous labor. See Eric Engen, Jane Gravelle, and Kent Smetters, "Dynamic Tax Models: Why They Do the Things They Do," *National Tax Journal*, Vol. 50, September, 1997, pp. 657-682.

Conclusion: Are Intertemporal Models Helpful or Harmful In Determining Feedback Effects?

Economists were attracted to intertemporal models because they were dissatisfied with the ad hoc treatment of savings in Solow models. However, intertemporal models are far less transparent, and modelers appear in some cases to make little attempt to connect the elasticities associated with labor supply to the ones found in empirical evidence. The JCT model has come close but, as illustrated, it is possible to come even closer to matching the empirical evidence, while at the same time minimizing "shooting in the dark" with a labor supply response to the interest rate. JCT also incorporates life cycle elements in their MEG model that do not involve labor supply responses to rates of return. Nevertheless, the assumption of equal substitution elasticities between consumption across far apart periods means that these models still rest on unproven, and probably unreasonable assumptions about the elasticity of substitution between consumption amounts that are ten or twenty years apart. There is a question of whether intertemporal models do more harm than good, at least with respect to the feedback effects during the budget horizon, especially when parameter choices may induce a large labor supply response to the rate of return.

Intertemporal modelers presenting the background on their models sometimes report the first two values in **Table 4** but no measure of the leisure share of time, which makes it impossible to evaluate on the basis of their published work.[75] Sometimes even the minimal information on elasticities is not provided. (JCT and CBO report all their relevant assumptions.) Without the parameters to understand the models (and particularly without information on the time endowment), these models become impossible to evaluate or compare.

---

[75] Even accomplished modelers Diamond and Zodrow do not report this value in their latest work. See John W. Diamond and George R. Zodrow "Promoting Growth, Maintaining Progressivity, and Dealing with the Fiscal Crisis: CGE Simulations of a Temporary VAT Used for Debt Reduction," *Public Finance Review*, vol. 41, no. 6 November, 2013, pp. 852-884. They chose a value of 0.4 for the IES and 0.8 for the intratemporal substitution elasticity.

Appendix. A Simple Model of Feedback Effects

Consider a model which incorporates a labor supply based on an estimated elasticity of E. In that case, with L as labor, W as wages and t as the tax rate on wages (denoting a "d" as a change, so that dL is a small change in L and dL/L is a percentage change in L), the labor supply can be defined as:

(1) $dL/L = E(dW/W - dt/(1-t))$

This model assumes that E is positive, so labor rises with an increase in W and falls with an increase in t. Also note that the response is not to a percentage change in t, but to a percentage change in the after tax share, (1-t).

With this information, a simple revenue feedback effect can be estimated. Revenue from the tax is tWL and the change in revenue is:

(2) $d(tWL) = dt(WL) + tW(dL)$

Holding wages constant (this assumption will subsequently be relaxed), and substituting from (1) into (2), the ratio of the second term in (2) to the first (the feedback effect) is:

(3) $(tWdL)/((dt)WL) = -Et/(1-t)$

Assuming a tax rate of 25% and a labor supply elasticity of 0.1 to 0.2, the feedback effect ranges from 3.3% to 6.6%. The feedback effect is larger the larger the initial tax and the larger the elasticity.

A decrease in labor supply looking only at the labor market would be expected to raise wages which would affect the wage base and also have a feedback effect on labor. The rise in wages and the contraction in labor would also increase the rate of return to capital. This in turn could cause an increase in the capital stock (either from savings or from capital flows from abroad). To address these effects in the short run, the model would also require a production function which shows how labor and capital can be combined.

Every model has a "numeraire" or a fixed value since economic effects depend on relative, rather than absolute, values. A sensible numeraire for this model is the overall price level, P. Changes in prices are a weighted average of the wage and rate of return depending on their share of income. Setting the share of capital income as a, and denoting the rate of return as R and the capital stock as K (to keep the model simply, depreciation is not included and income shares reflect net product):

(4) $dP/P = a(dR/R) + (1-a) dW/W = 0$

Finally consider a common production function (a Cobb Douglas) that has the characteristic that income shares are fixed, so that a is a constant and:

(5) $RK/WL = a/(1-a)$

When this equation is differentiated to convert it into percentage changes;

(6) dR/R +dK/K-dW/W-dL/L= 0

If K is constant, substitute from (4) to eliminate dR/R. From equation (1):

(7) (td(WL))/(dtWL) = [E(1-a)t]/[(1-t)(1+aE)]

The feedback response from the labor tax, assuming a is 0.25, is smaller. Rather than 3.3% to 6.6%, it is 2.4% to 4.8%.

If capital income is also subject to tax, then the effects of the rise in R needs to also be calculated and taken into account. If taxed at the same rate, the result is [Eat]/[(1-t)(1+aE)], which is 0.8% to 1.6%. Adding both responses = [Et]/[(1-t)(1+aE)]. As this example indicates, with an across the board tax the feedback effects are not much different incorporating these general equilibrium effects (3.2% and 6.4% rather than 3.3% and 6.6%).

These results can also be used to show increases in output. In the case where the capital stock is fixed, the percentage change in labor for a given percentage change in the after tax share is the same as the feedback effect in (3) but since labor is only a part of output, it would be multiplied by the output share (0.75). The result is the same as the ratio in (7). Thus a 20% decrease in the tax rate would increase output, with an elasticity of 0.1, by 2.4% times 0.2, or 0.5% percent. For the 0.2 elasticity the result would be 1%.

The previous short run model had a fixed capital stock and three variables, the rate of return R, the wage rate W and the labor supply, L. A Solow growth model allows (if it is a closed economy) growth over time in capital and feedback effects. In the long run, that permits a change in capital. Capital can grow not only because of a change in savings rate but also because increased labor income generates capital to go along with it even if the savings rate does not change.

In the long run steady state, additional variables, output (Q) and the savings rate (s) have to be added.

(8) dQ/Q = adK/K +(1-a)dL/L

which indicates that the percentage change in output is a weighted average of the percentage changes in capital and labor.

In addition the savings rate is determined by the after tax return, where t_k is the tax rate on capital income.

(9) ds/s = Es (dR/R-dt_k/(1-t_k))

Finally, in the steady state savings equals investment,

 (10) gK = sQ

where g is a constant exogenous growth rate of population and technology. Thus,

(11) dK/K = ds/s + dQ/Q

These results are shown in **Table 1** and **Table 2**, for various elasticities.

The feedback effects, which all have the same denominator: $1+aE+(1-a)Es$, and are all multiplied by $t/(1-t)$ have the following numerators:

(A) Labor tax change with general income tax in place: $E(1+Es)$

(B) Capital income tax change with general income tax in place: $Es(1+E)$

(C) Income tax change (on capital and labor): $(1-a)E(1+Es) +aEs(1+E)$

Output effects can also be calculated for the solutions to the change in labor and capital as $(1-a) dL/L+adK/K$.

Author Contact Information

Jane G. Gravelle
Senior Specialist in Economic Policy
jgravelle@crs.loc.gov, 7-7829